My Family and Other Poems

An Anthology

To Jo
with best wishes
Gillian.

Gillian Grinham

Copyright 2014 by Gillian Grinham
First published in 2014 by
Milton Contact Ltd

A CIP catalogue record for this book is available from The British Library

ISBN: 978-0-9929289-1-9

All rights reserved. No part of this publication may be reproduced, stored in a retrieval system, or transmitted in any form or by any means – electronic, mechanical, photocopy, recording, or any other – except for brief quotations in print reviews, without prior permission of the author.

Printed in the United Kingdom

Milton Contact Ltd
3 Hall End, Milton, Cambridge, UK
CB24 6AQ
www.miltoncontact.co.uk

Contents

Contents... iii

Ward F4 1

   Two Lists 3
   Patient Report 4
   Night 2, 2AM 5
   Night 3, 4AM 6
   Drug Round 7
   Drug Addict 7
   Day 5 – Patient Report (1) 8
   Day 5 Patient Report (2) 9
   Country Mile – Or a Walk to the Loo 10
   Plugged In 11
   The Next Bed 11
   Haute Couture 12

Harry 13

   Harry, Two Days Old 15
   To H.J.E.G. 16
   For Harry (who's Two) 17
   For Harry – Who's Three 18

Four is More!!	20
It's Cool To Be FIVE!	21
For Harry, now he is Six!	22
Seven	24

Joseph 25

Joseph	27
For Joseph Now He Is One	28
Two!!Who?	29
Who Is Two?	30
Who Is Three?	31
Where is Joey?	33
Joey is FIVE!	34

Boys at Large 35

Waiting for Christmas	37
Patient Rabbit	38
Silly Rhymes For Sensible Boys	39
Rabbit on Holiday	40
More Silly Rhymes for even More Sensible Boys	41
Lost Seconds	42

Holidays 45

Thai Morning	47
Laos Evening	49

The Mekong	50
Journey	51
The Morning Sun?	51
Summer Holidays	52

The Daughter Down Under 53

Australian Birthday 1	55
Australian Birthday 2	56
After the Chocolates	57

Celebrations 61

For Eileen	63
Ode To Phil	66
Rose	68
Perfect Pitch	69

The Classroom and Beyond 71

Sonnet to JA	73
Monday Afternoons	74
English Litriture or Musings of an Invigilator	75
False Alarm	76
Reflection	77
Time	78
Personal Achievement	79

Two Special Days	81
Wedding Day	83
Anniversary	84
Hymns	85
A Mother's Lullaby	87
Wedding Anniversary Hymn	89
Christening Hymn	90
Christening Hymn	91

Ward F4

Two Lists

The pamphlet says
'Things to bring;
Flannel, toothbrush, soap,
Night-clothes and
Easy day-clothes.'
Practical things.

But grandma's list says:
'Photos, cards, book
And, most important of all
An owl, a squirrel
And...
Love, hugs and kisses from two very special boys.'
Essential, personal things.

Patient Report

The nurses say I'm stable.
That's not quite true, I fear.
My knees are really painful,
I have to make that clear!

I'm trying not to make a fuss,
Or let my sadness show.
These knees are not so happy,
I thought I'd let you know.

There's an answer to my problem,
It's the only thing to do.
I need to come home right away –
I need to be with you!

Night 2, 2AM

7 times and 5 times ring their bells,
simultaneously.
After a morphine-dozy day, I am awake –
A guilty, catheter-smug listener behind my
curtains.
'I need a wee!' This is 5 times, alias
13/03/43.
The dialogue covers the now-familiar territory,
'I've a numb bum and the oxygen makes my
nose sore.'
I switch to 7 times, where Spain is meeting
Thetford,
Unsuccessfully.
'What did you have done?'
'Would I like a bun?'
'Where's the pain?'
'Can I bend what?'
Spain gives up, defeated, takes blood pressure
silently.
Now wide awake, I try some exercises,
Determined to get home to my tranquil
bedroom.
Then it hits me –
7 times and 5 times have been placed – by the
Physios
To make me do just that!

Night 3, 4AM

We've had a pretty peaceful night,
The patients in Bay Three.
We hardly used our buzzers
Two hips, two knees
And me.

Knee One asked for a bed-pan,
Hip One zimmered to the loo.
The other two were restless.
And me – what did I do?

Well – I wrote another poem,
Not stressful, you'll agree.
Yes, a pretty peaceful night
For Two Hips, Two Knees
And me.

Drug Round

'Marks out of 10 for your pain?' asks Nurse,
Cheerfully brandishing the longed-for phial.
'You know – 1 bearable, 10 unbearable.'
But I am a teacher,
I give marks out of 10 for:
Homework, exam questions, small essays.
Silently I shout
'JUST GIVE ME THE MORPHINE!'
Aloud, politely
'6'
Then a rebel makes me add
'And three quarters.'

Drug Addict

Warfarin jabs hurt my stomach,
Morphine makes me sick,
I can't pronounce the other pills,
The Paracetamol's big as a brick!

Day 5 – Patient Report (1)

13/10/45 has become institutionalised.
6.15 – left arm raised obediently for intra-venous anti-sickness.
6.30 – right arm raised for BP, left finger for pulse, forehead temperature.
Can even identify the 3 'remainders' with eyes shut:
'Shuffle, shuffle, clunk, clunk wheeze'
That's the Right Hip Verbal Diarrhoearist
(Best avoidance tactic – feigned sleep)
'Glide, glide, sigh' =
Right Knee, stripped vein – sane, hooray!
Loud snores, bed-pan apologies, occasional whimper =
Left Knee, deaf, 87,
Communication tactics – nods and smiles!
(NB look up Aunt/Mother in Dickens)
But what of 2 half-knees and catheter?
All she can do is scribble – and wait
For 4 o'clock!

Day 5 Patient Report (2)

Skills acquired:
Ankle wiggling technique – excellent.
Buttock clenching routine – superb.
Manual dexterity with bed controls – good.
Identifying staff accents – improving.
But...
Eating, standing, sitting – poor.
Walking – null points!

Verdict: must try harder.

Country Mile – Or a Walk to the Loo

(Apologies to Slim Dusty)

I don't want to run a marathon
Or win the Wightman Cup,
I simply want to stand and sit
Without always throwing up.

I've always had my little lists
Of things I'd like to do,
But the trip I'd really like to take
Is a visit to the loo!

So when my head stops spinning round
And settles for a while,
I'll grab the wheely walking frame
And walk that country mile!

Then the ringers from the Top End
And my mate the Baldy Bay
And the Court of King Caractacus
Will cheer and shout 'hooray'!

Plugged In

Forget Stickpeople,
I'm Tubeperson.
Five shiny, spaghetti tubes:
Two export the badness,
Three import goodness.

Perhaps the world would change
If we could plug ourselves in at night,
Letting the
Badness out and the goodness in!

The Next Bed

Please turn her out in the long yard,
Please find her a nice baldy bay,
Please take her away from my bedside –
I don't want to hear her today!

I shall conquer the pain and the sickness,
I shall soon walk the loo country mile,
But I'll burst out with rage and frustration
If she doesn't SHUT UP for a while!

Haute Couture

I've given up putting on knickers,
There's no point wearing a bra,
I've a catheter stuck in my vitals
And I won't be going that far.
The tubes in my arms means it's T-shirts,
Keen slippers are wedged on my feet,
But I'm washed and I'm dressed – of a fashion,
And at last, here I am, in my seat!

Harry

Harry, Two Days Old

The hollow in my shoulder
Is still warm where your dark head nestled
As you snuggled against me
While we shared those peaceful moments
together.
However, you are not the first to rest there,
Two little copper heads, many years ago
Nuzzled as they, too, were comforted.
But today that warmth has come from you
In the hollow of my shoulder.

To H.J.E.G.

The Twelfth of May is a special day,
A happy day,
A Hip-Hip-Hooray day!!

There will be noise
Of girls and boys,
And lots of toys!

And the star of the show,
What does he know?
'It's fun to be one,'
Says Harry.

For Harry (who's Two)

It's a wonderful day for our Harry – he's TWO!
He jumps out of bed saying 'What shall I do?
I could pick up a stick and a bright shiny ball
And have fun playing hockey in both lounge and hall.
Then I'll stand with my bat in front of the wicket
And hit lots of runs in a fast game of cricket.
Then I'll snuggle up close in a big comfy chair
With Mummy and Daddy and Boydie, my bear,
Reading books about farms, ducks and tractors galore,
Then I'll sit at my table and find things to draw.
So, you see, there are so many things I can do,
And I'm feeling so happy!' says Harry (he's TWO).

For Harry – Who's Three

Can't stop!
I'm busy!
There's a world out there to explore, you see,
There are so many things to do when you're
THREE!
I'm hunting a Stegasaurus,
Has he passed this way,
Looking for his prey?
I'm hunting a Stegasaurus.
Can't stop!
I'm busy!
I'm looking for a woodlouse.
I've asked little Joe,
But I'm sure he doesn't know.
I'm looking for a woodlouse.
Can't stop!
I'm busy!
I'm searching for a ladybird,
I'm going to count her spots,
She's hiding in those pots,
I'm searching for a ladybird.
Can't stop!
I'm busy!

I'm digging for some worms!
I like it when they wriggle –
It makes me scream and giggle!
I'm digging for some worms.
Can't stop!
I'm busy!
There's a world out there to explore, you see,
There are so many things to do when you're
THREE!!

Four is More!!

Harrygersaurus and Josephusadocus
Are lively little boys!
They love to run and jump and play
And make a happy noise.

Harrygersaurus and Josephusdocus
Are busy little boys!
They love to draw and paint and read
And make a quieter noise.

Harrygersaurus and Josephusdocus
Are happy little boys!
Big H has reached the age of FOUR!!
Let's all make lots of **NOISE!!**

It's Cool To Be FIVE!

He can spot a red kite
When it flies overhead.
He can count to two hundred
When lying in bed.
He spots woodlice and ants
As they crawl on the ground.
He can make Joey happy
By jumping around!
He's the Dinosaur expert –
The crab-catching Star!
'Pass the Pigs', 'Shear the Sheep'
He's the winner by far!
He's the happiest boy
Who's alert and alive,
He's cool and he's bouncy –
He's Harry – he's FIVE!!

For Harry, now he is Six!

HOORAY, HOORAY, HOORAY, HOORAY!

AND WHAT OTHER WORD WAS I GOING TO SAY?

RACKING MY BRAINS FOR A SUITABLE RHYME,

ROLLING THE WORDS IN MY HEAD ALL THE TIME,

YELLING, 'THAT'S IT!' ON A WALK THROUGH THE TOWN,

GRABBING A PENCIL TO WRITE IT ALL DOWN.

READING EACH LINE MAKING SURE IT'S NOT BAD,

IGNORING POOR GRANDAD WHO'S LOOKING QUITE SAD.

NEARING THE BIG DAY WITH LITTLE TO WRITE,

HOPING THE WORDS WILL APPEAR IN THE NIGHT!

ASTOUNDING MYSELF – I'VE GOT SOMETHING TO SAY!!

MAKING THIS POEM ONE LONG, **BIG**

HOORAY!!!

Seven

There is a boy in Icknield Way
Who simply loves to run and play.
At football, he's the one to score,
Then see him dash and go for more!
He's now enjoying playing cricket,
He hits balls strongly at the wicket,
And as a fielder – watch him run.
For Harry, sport is such good fun!
He's SEVEN today, his friends are here,
It's a football tournament this year!

Joseph

Joseph

You are
The beloved, missing part of the family jigsaw.
You are
The cherished reward for a Mother's night of pain and anguish.
You are
The perfect miracle of a Father's anxious waiting.
You are
The Piston Cup for a proud and loving Brother.
You are
Another blessing for joyful, thankful Grandparents.
You are
Joseph.

For Joseph Now He Is One

Who is always on the go?
Our Joe!
Who goes fast and never slow?
Our Joe!
Who loves giggles with his brother,
And cuddles with his mother,
Who is ONE today,
Let's shout 'Hooray!'
For...our...JOE!!!

Two!!Who?

Who's that springing off the chairs?
Who's that climbing up the stairs?
Who loves to shout and bellow?
Whose favourite colour's yellow?
It's Joe, that's who -
Our Joseph now is TWO!!

Just see him bounce, bounce, jump!
Just hear him crash, bang, bump!
He's England's ginger fan,
He's our Special Birthday Man!
It's Joe, that's who –
Our Joseph now is TWO!!

Who Is Two?

Harry's little brother, Joe,
Is now no longer new.
He's not a baby any more,
And that's because he's TWO!!

Harry's little brother, Joe,
Is now no longer new.
He always loves to kick a ball,
And that's because he's TWO!!

'I'm not a little brother,
And I'm certainly not new!
I can do all sorts of things,'
Says Joseph, who is TWO!!

Who Is Three?

He likes to run and jump about,
And when he's cross he likes to shout!

Let's all cheer for Joseph
Who sailed on the sea.
He's bouncy'
He's ginger,
He's happy, He's THREE!!

He sometimes likes to munch a sweet,
His smile's the cheekiest you will meet!

Let's all cheer for Joseph
Who sailed on the sea.
He's bouncy,
He's ginger,
He's happy,
He's THREE!!

He greets us with a hug and kiss,
His birthday's one you must not miss!

Let's all cheer for Joseph
Who sailed on the sea.
He's bouncy,
He's ginger,
He's happy,
He's THREE!!

Where is Joey?

He's not out in the garden
Hitting a ball,
He's not rolling lorries and cars
Down the hall.
He's not eating Kit-Kat,
Or munching a pear,
We've searched and we've searched,
But he's simply not there!

Then the lounge curtain twitches,
So we then take a look –
And there is our Joey-
'I've been reading a book.
But I'll come out and play,
There's so much to explore,
Life is fun and exciting –
I'm so happy I'm FOUR!!'

Joey is FIVE!

His run-up seems like half a mile,
His bowling action makes us smile.
He hits the ball – it goes for four,
He swipes again, and scores some more.
With racket steady in his hand
He hits the ball and sees it land
Perfectly within the court.
Our Joey really loves his sport.
In Mrs Oakley's class this year
He reads and writes so well, we hear.
And now he's FIVE - oh goodness me!
I'm sure he'll eat some cake for tea!

Boys at Large

Waiting for Christmas

There are not many weeks to go
Till Harry and his brother Joe
Hang Christmas stockings on their door
And look for hoof prints on the floor!
For reindeer pulling Santa's sleigh
Will surely ride down Icknield Way.
But this year, when they come to call
They'll find a notice on the wall,
Pinned clearly by a coloured marker:
'The boys have gone to Nanny Parker!'
So up into the sky they'll climb
To make sure they arrive on time
And give to our two special boys
Their presents – books and sweets and toys!

Patient Rabbit

Why is Joey crying?
Why is Mummy sighing?
Why is Harry searching through the house?
Has Joey lost a slipper?
Has Daddy flipped a kipper?
Is Boydie hiding somewhere with a mouse?
No! Rabbit's done a runner.
We know he's not a stunner
All floppy legs and ears and stripey vest.
But in Joey's special place
Snuggled neatly on his face
Rabbit's Number 1 – he's just the Best!
But don't worry, all comes right,
He's been a patient for the night
At the hospital they went the previous day.
Now he's back with Joe at last,
All tears and sadness past,
And everyone can cheer and shout HOORAY!!

Silly Rhymes For Sensible Boys

There once was a bramble called Pete
Who wrapped himself round Grandma's feet.
She fell on her face
In a very wet place.
All the bramble could say,
'That was neat1'

In a field there were two busy men,
They were called Farmer Bert and young Ben.
They were making a list
Of the cows they had missed,
When a voice shouted 'Stop!'
Count AGAIN!'

A skilful young striker, HG,
Was practising right by the sea.
Along comes young Joe,
Saying' 'Let's have a go,'
And kicks the ball
Into a tree!

A meerkat was peering around
When he heard an unusual sound.
He looked left and right,
And he then had a fright
As a snake slithered by
On the ground!

Mr Bean was once baking a cake
When his mixing bowl started to break,
The sticky gunge slithered
While Mr Bean dithered.
Oh dear, that's another
Mistake!!

Rabbit on Holiday

There once was a floppy-eared rabbit
Who developed a wandering habit.
He landed in France
And snatched at his chance,
Saying, 'This Formula One I'll inhabit!'

More Silly Rhymes for even More Sensible Boys

Grandad and Grandma are coming to Tring.
They've not come to dance,
And they've not come to sing.
They may read a book,
Cook a meal,
Kick a ball.
But they're seeing their Grandsons,
And that's best of all!

What a funny name is TRING!
It's like a bird about to sing,
Or a bell that just goes 'Ting'.
In your wild imagining,
Would you like to live in PING?

Lost Seconds

'I only turned away for a second when...'
The little fingers let go of the kite.
Away it flew
Over the railway line, into the bush
Leaving
Tears for big brother,
Problems for Grandad.

'I only turned away for a second when...'
The little fist wielded the felt-tip,
Painting T-shirt, vest,
And round pink tummy,
Leaving
Washing for Mummy,
Bathing for Grandma.

'I only turned away for a second when...'
Little feet took their owner
Through the gate, up the drive
And away down the road,
Leaving
Panic for parents,
Frenzy for friends.

'We only turned away for a second when...'
The kite-throwing,
Body-painting
Ginger escapee
Reached his second birthday
Leaving us all wondering
'Where did all those seconds go?'

Holidays

Thai Morning

The mist rises -
A workman, passive, immobile, waits under a palm tree.

The mist rises -
Flames lick the black cooking pot,
The first meal of the day tended by the squatting woman,
While the family wait under the bamboo roof.

The mist rises –
A dog yawns, scratches, ambles to his place by the road.

The mist rises –
The lurching truck turns into the school yard,
Its cargo of laughing children spill over the sides, the back.

The mist rises –
The sack of oranges dwarfs the young woman,
Slowly making her way down the hill
Toddler in front, baby cocooned at her breast.

The mist rises —
Three saffron-robed priests approach the temple,
The golden Buddha catching the first gleams of the orange sun
Which now takes over from the mist,
Warming and lighting the new Thai day.

While we —
Isolated within our air-conditioned cube,
Gaze, savouring every detail,
Harvesting each moment like grains of rice,
To be stored for nourishment and comfort
During a cold, bleak, English winter.

Laos Evening

Two gamelan notes are struck –
Three long strings are plucked and strummed
– A single drumbeat –
Then all combine to create
A gentle, haunting tune.

Two rows of kneeling dancers,
Their silk costumes a bright contrast
With the dark palms behind,
Giggle, adjust their sashes and start to clap.

One girl, though, morose, refusing to deliver
the obligatory smile,
Instead looks down, plays with her mobile
phone.
The teachers in the audience nod to each
other,
'That one's trouble,' their shared glances say.
But, two tunes later,
With rhythmic swaying and expressive hands
She is transformed,
As ancient tribal dances come alive
In young, slim feet.
And once again the West is awed and
humbled
Under an Oriental spell.

The Mekong

Needing no visas, no travel documents,
It winds its relentless way
From distant foothills of Tibet
To its many-fingered delta,
Ignoring all border crossings.
It is both friend and foe.
Slicing in two the dense, impenetrable jungle.
Long bamboo poles,
Precariously placed on jagged rocks,
Give testament to a slippery, finned harvest.
An economic force,
Flat-bottomed boats transport cargo –
Rice, wood, tourists,
Down its brown highway.
But, come the monsoon,
Gorged and sated, it overpowers sandbanks,
Licks the jungle fringe,
Taunting stilt-dwelling villagers
Whose boats negotiate tortuous, winding paths
Between visible and invisible hazards.
A brown, pulsing artery,
It will survive
When both stilt-dwellers and tourists
Have gone.

Journey

Dad drives the car with practised ease,
Mum has the map upon her knees.
She thinks she knows the route – but wait,
What makes it hard to concentrate
On fleeting road-signs all the time
Is that she's searching for a rhyme!

The Morning Sun?

'We'll have the door just over here,'
Said Dad, in camping mood.
'Yes, dear,' said Mum, a little vague,
Her mind on drink and food.
They put in poles, and hammered pegs –
They worked with might and main.
It didn't really matter,
In the morning came – the rain!!

Summer Holidays

Watch out, crabs and lizards,
Our Harry's on the prowl.
He's spotted cranes and egrets,
He's heard the evening owl.
He loves to hunt in rock pools
Giving every stone a glance.
He's having such a lovely time
On holiday in France.

The Daughter Down Under

Australian Birthday 1

Possums are warm, Possums are wise,
Possums have bulging, luminous eyes.
They scramble on wires, just over your head,
And scamper in attics while you lie in bed.
Today they feel festive – and we both know why,
It's Ginger Poms' birthday –
So Possums say 'Hi!'

Australian Birthday 2

If it's autumn here in England
Then it's summer down in Oz.
But they celebrate in every place
And shout 'Hooray' because
It's daughter Rachel's birthday,
The best time of the year,
And everyone is jolly,
(Mum sheds a little tear).
We hope she will be happy,
We know she won't be sad,
For Mum and Dad send all their love,
And that makes Rachel glad!

After the Chocolates

Rhyming couplets are suitable for Harry now he's six,
But sophisticated rhyme and Joseph simply do not mix.
But what's the mode for Rachel who has chosen to exist
In a country that's so far away and oh – how much she's missed!
I've decided to experiment with genre, form and style,
And choose the one most suitable and ponder all the while
On a ginger girl (with freckles) cuddling Pooh Bear in her bed
Who now stalks the hallowed corridors of distant ANZ.
So...here...goes...

Yes, I remember Ansteystrop –
Only the – hot platform where
Lots of people come and go
Not talking of Michelangelo.
Faster than fairies, faster than witches

Is Rachel peddling on her way to work.
Once more unto the breach, dear accountants,
It is a far, far better thing that we do now,
Into the Valley of Death
Where sleeps the crimson petal.
To be, or not to be
Halfway down the stairs,
That is the question.
Or when shall we three meet again?
One thing puzzles me –
What is this life, if, full of care
We have no time to stand and stare
Over the hills and far away;
But then a star danced
In the tulgy wood.
Amid a host of daffodils
She saw the water lily bloom
In a bed of delphiniums blue and geraniums red.
Hail to thee, blithe spirit,
Shall I compare thee to a summer's day?
Out, out, vile jelly, out damned spot,
Dashing away with the smoothing iron,
With twinkling brown eyes.

Down by the station, early in the morning,
Our revels now are ended.
Fear no more the heat of the sun.
It is a truth, universally acknowledged
That a ginger-haired, cycle-riding, hockey-playing,
Veg-growing daughter is
Much loved, and much missed.

Celebrations

For Eileen

Keep it neat, keep it simple,
Clean-cut lines – no fuss
But shrieks of delight when the red-hatted gentleman
Alights on the Christmas beach from his pontoon sleigh.
An early fashion victim, scar from glass beads glinting in the sun, runs to greet him.
Sisters, sisters, always such…
Up to mischief sisters. One minute, still figures in bunk beds,
Then…tickle and scratch until sleep stops all games.

Keep it neat, keep it simple,
Clean-cut lines – no fuss
But summertime tricks
Not Cathy's Clown, but sister acrobats,
Whirling away the holiday hours.
No fuss, though when cruel wire cut short
The scrumping sisters' secret jaunt.

Keep it neat, keep it simple,
Clean-cut lines – no fuss
But

The lure of the bop-bop beat,
Walking or running back to happiness,
Now Strictly Come Dancing sisters,
Keep it neat – the hand ready to stay the
swinging middy.
Fashion victim again –
The bottled sun emerged a vivid orange.

Keep it neat, keep it simple,
Clean-cut lines – no fuss
But
Sisters, partners in fun and dance
Find new roles, fresh exploits.
Washing machines produce clean-cut lines,
Bowls of salad keep it simple,
A little girl keeps it neat, with ribbons and
costume matching.

Keep it neat, keep it simple,
Clean-cut lines – no fuss
But
NO WAY
For two tiny figures have dared to challenge
Those rules of living.
With irresistible persistence
They have pushed back the boundaries.
Nothing neat, nothing simple,
Always fuss, nothing clean.

But their trim, elegant, fun-loving
Grandmother,
The little sister, always young,
Loves them, and is hugged and loved in
return.

(for Eileen Parker on her sixtieth birthday)

Ode To Phil

Let us go then, you and I, On the Wings of a Dove
To View *A Portrait of a Lady.*
Earth has not anything to show more fair
Than Phil, in the early morning sun,
Sitting on *This Royal Throne of Kings,*
Ignoring the busy highway,
Soaking up equal portions of sun and cereal,
(Waft, waft ye winds)
Wrapped in her dressing gown
And morning thoughts of beaches in South Africa
And essays to be completed, books to read.
O what is that sound that so thrills the ear?
It is the early morning call of two students,
Caroline and Phil, loudly organising their day ahead.
Lectures over, *the winter evening settles down,*
But not our Phil, '*On with the dance,*' she cries,
And in bare feet she dances to *the light fantastic.*
Come nine o'clock, it's time for 'Friends',
But with Phil it's always time for friends,
She is *Our Mutual Friend,*
The one who cares, the one who listens,

But one wild midnight,
Phil and her friends were *Phantoms of delight*
As Lloyds Bank became transported to
A moonlit, and nude, campus!
Student life over, *To be, or not to be?*
Bikini-clad Phil's roads led to Spain – more sun, more cereal.
Eventually, feelings of *O to be in England*
Overtook 'Viva Espana'.
Phil's *heart leapt up when* she *beheld*
The Advert in The Times.
'A PR's life for me,' she cried.
As ever, the ingredients of life to Phil were
Friends, fun and laughter.
Until...
It is a truth universally acknowledged that

The cry *Come live with me and be my love*
Would not unheeded go by
Someone so attractive, loving and caring
As our Phil.
But *Sigh no more, ladies, sigh no more*,
Our lives will never ever be 'unPhilled'.

(For Phil on her thirtieth birthday)

Rose

A Rose brings joy
To a dull, gloomy day.
A Rose adds colour
In a plain, sombre world.
A fragrant Rose lifts
A roomful of drooping spirits.
A Rose is a symbol
Of family love.
Happy Birthday, Rose!!

(for Rose Ornbo, on her seventieth birthday)

Perfect Pitch

We've led you a merry dance, over the years,
Through crescendos and diminuendos.
We've hemiolad our way,
Tripping with our voices most lightly
April evenings, in all seasons.
Through torrents in summer, calm evenings with a rosy glow,
We've charmed audiences asleep with our delicious numbers.
Our hearts were inditing as we travelled
Through Afton Water, taking in Scarborough and Widdecombe Fairs en route.
Always in stately dress, or frocks, we assembled,
Ceasing our chatter, chatter,
We banished sorrow, banished care.
Come Christmas, we rocked and wassailed, full of figgy pudding,
In three ships, always following the star.
With drummers drumming, bells ringing,
We were the seraph choir singing.
Sometimes rallentandoes ignoring, pauses unheeding,
Chaos ensued – but Hallelujah,

Under your skilful baton,
Music won the Day!
And so, tutti, in unison, in triple fff and
appassionato,
We say thanks, Maestro,
For times full of harmony, melody and fun.

(for James Recknell, choirmaster of Culford
Choral Society)

The Classroom and Beyond

Sonnet to JA

When looking fondly at the classroom wall
I read a name that conjures up delight.
While other writers' learned works soon pall,
This author's scribbling summon up a sight
Of elegance and lives so keenly spent
Within the narrow confines of a town.
The wars could rage – peace treaties could be rent –
She wrote of hats, the fashion of a gown,
Arrival of a curate, or a harp,
The acquisition of a carriage or a cart.
These things seem trivial – readers sometimes carp,
But truly – her main subject was…the heart!
Let fire and tempest rage, if still remain
The golden, matchless work of well-loved Jane.

Monday Afternoons

We came each Monday, beady-eyed and keen,
Eager to read and learn from works of those
Who'd reached the dizzy heights of published prose.
The time arrived for our work to be seen
And let our tutor add that extra sheen
To characters and genre that we chose
And to each chapter's opening and close.
Verbal excess was purged - our work looked lean.
Topics and thoughts ranged wide - our numbers, few.
Our wings we feel are spreading, every one.
The weeks flew by, our novels slowly grew.
We've reached week twelve, all exercises done,
And so, our tutor, praise and thanks to you.
We've written, read and talked – and had such fun.

(for Caron Freeborn, my MA tutor at ARU)

English Litriture or Musings of an Invigilator

Nothing could be grimmer
Than staring at Tim Rimmer
As he tries to muddle through his Plath and Hughes.
I'd rather sing a medley
Than contemplate Tim Gredley
Whose brains are slowly sinking to his shoes.
And what about James Scarff?
He'd be better off by half
Running up and down the pitch and having fun!
And to woeful Johnnie Sims
They might as well be hymns
Those poems that he's reading, one by one.
I'm afraid I know what Clark
Will be getting for his mark
Even though his books appear well-thumbed.
And as for Tommy French
He'll be sitting on the bench
In spite of all the depths that he has plumbed.
And look at beefy Fraser,
I think you'll need a laser

To penetrate exactly what he means.
And as for scholar Brinkley –
I'd rather take a bus to Hinkley
Than peruse his random thoughts on all those scenes!

(All these pupils are now well-respected, conscientious young men!)

False Alarm

'Call out the men,' said Fireman Bill.
'The alarm's gone off in Muswell Hill.'
'Chill out, you guys, what's all the fuss?'
Said Matt, just ambling to his bus.
'While I was reading all my post,
I only went and burnt the toast!'

Reflection

The train has stopped – temporarily.
'This journey seemed short,' the passengers say with surprise,
Forgetting they said that last year.
Some look tired, some impatient, others excited,
But all are ready for this lull in the ride.

Time to reflect on the journey past,
Time to stretch their legs, to take on refreshment,
See other places.

Not all passengers, however, will return to the carriages.
They have other journeys, alternative routes.
Farewells will be said - but they will carry with them
The priceless luggage of memory.

Soon the train will move on, other new passengers
Are waiting at the next station,
But for now, and for all,
The train has stopped.

Time

Yesterday.
What is yesterday?
Once it was tomorrow – a planned for
Hoped for,
Excitedly waited for – day.
But always – a day in the future.

Then tomorrow became today,
Ready to be filled with – our plans,
Hopes,
Excitedly, anxiously,
At last – a day in the present.

Now today has become yesterday,
Plans and hopes become memories of things
accomplished
Things achieved.
Excitement and anxiety become experience.
Memory and experience – these are
yesterday's gifts
For today and tomorrow.

Personal Achievement

'Well done!'
'Gold Star!'
'Smiley Face!'
'Merit Prize!'
'The whole team played well!'

Pink with pride
We acknowledge praise,
Collect the certificate, the team medal,
Stumbling, embarrassed, we return to our seat.

In time, certificates yellow with age,
Medals gather dust,
Smiley faces peel off.
But nothing can remove
The giddy, exhilarating feeling of delight
When we reached and achieved our very own,
personal goal.

Two Special Days

Wedding Day

Your wedding is a day of joy,
Your wedding is a day of happiness,
Your wedding is a day of love.
Together we bring our gifts
Of friendship,
Good wishes,
And love.

But this is only the start,
These are only the tools,
The essentials of your journey.

Together you will add
Your youth,
Your laughter,
And your love.

And when you bind all these with hope,
When you weave into these your trust,
Together you will have created
A marriage.

(For Sarah and Matthew April 10th 2004)

Anniversary

Happy Ruby Sunday!
But – why ruby? Why red?
I can understand silver, gold, diamond,
Precious metals, long-service awards,
But red?
Red roses, red hearts,
Clichés both.
Perhaps 'red rag to a bull', or 'you make me see red,'
Appropriate for forty?
Maybe - those familiar, well worn needles of irritation,
Unsheathed to provoke at extreme moments,
Retracted with relief when the skirmish passes.
But red for the bloodline we two created,
Whose future we ponder
As we share the red glow of the home hearth.
Happy Ruby Sunday, my love!

(April 14th, 1973)

Hymns

A Mother's Lullaby

Who has come to visit the Baby?
Who has come to worship the King?
Shepherds arrive, invited by angels
To bring Him their presents, to play and to sing.

But Mary, His mother, tenderly watches,
Gazes at all things, gently apart.
She smiles at the shepherds, their presents and praises,
And ponders, ponders all things in her heart.

Who has come to worship the Baby?
Who has travelled from countries afar?
Wise Men arrive, bearing gifts full of meaning,
Their journeys were guided and led by a Star.

But Mary, His mother, tenderly watches,
Gazes at all things, gently apart.
She smiles at the Wise Men, their presents and praises,
And ponders, ponders all things in her heart.

Who will come to view the Redeemer?
Who will come to worship God's Son?
All are invited to pray to the Saviour,
And offer their hearts to the Lord's Holy One.

But Mary, His mother, tenderly watches,
Gazes at all things, gently apart.
She smiles at His people, their offerings and praises,
And ponders, ponders all things in her heart.

(Music for this carol was written by my friend and colleague, Nicholas Hopton. It was sung by the school choir at Culford School carol service in St Edmundsbury Cathedral)

Wedding Anniversary Hymn

We asked God to guide us in our future life,
We prayed for His blessing on husband and wife.
As we vowed to each other in God's Holy place
We knelt to receive both His love and His grace.

God has guided us gently, through laughter and tears,
He has blessed us and loved us through all hopes and fears.
Now we offer Him praise for a shared Christian life,
And we ask Him for blessing on husband and wife.

(tune: Stowey)

Christening Hymn

God created this world
And its gifts for us all.
He designed all its life,
All things large and those small.
He knows every creature
In earth, sea and land.
We are all of us cherished
In His loving hand.

We give thanks for this child
He has placed in our care,
Whom we ask God to bless
And protect in our prayer,
May he grow in the knowledge
That God is his guide,
As he travels through life,
God will be by his side.

(tune: Stowey)

(For the Christening of Harry John Edward Grinham, 15th October 2006)

Christening Hymn

In the creatures around us
God makes His clear mark,
From the dormouse and fox
To the whale and the shark.
We all have our place
In the world that we share,
And ask for His blessing
On all in God's care.

We commit these we love
To our Lord's tender care.
For protection and blessing
We offer our prayer.
May they grow in the knowledge
That God is their guide.
As they travel through life
God will be by their side.

(tune: Stowey)

(For the Christening of Sarah Grinham and Joseph George Lenton Grinham, September 2009)